Series 536

LADYBIRD BOOKS

UK | USA | Canada | Ireland | Australia | India | New Zealand | South Africa

Ladybird Books is part of the Penguin Random House group of companies whose addresses can be found at global.penguinrandomhouse.com.

www.penguin.co.uk www.puffin.co.uk www.ladybird.co.uk

Penguin Random House UK

First published 1960. This facsimile edition published 2018.

001

Printed in China

A CIP catalogue record for this book is available from the British Library

ISBN: 978–0–241–34826–0

All correspondence to:
Ladybird Books, Penguin Random House Children's
80 Strand, London WC2R 0RL

THE LADYBIRD BOOK OF

GARDEN FLOWERS

By

BRIAN VESEY-FITZGERALD, F.L.S.

Colour Illustrations by

JOHN LEIGH-PEMBERTON

Publishers: Wills & Hepworth Ltd., Loughborough

First published 1960

Forsythia A hardy shrub which grows to twelve feet and blooms early in the year. It should be planted in the autumn in well-tilled soil. After flowering, the old wood must be cut out to make room for the new, which will flower the following year.

Chionadoxa A member of the Lily family. It flowers early in the year; often at the same time as the snowdrops. It is a very good plant for rockeries. Plant the bulbs in the autumn, three inches apart and one inch deep.

Christmas Rose This is not a rose, but a Hellebore. It is called the " Christmas Rose " because it is often in flower on Christmas Day. It should be planted in September in the shade. The best place is under the branches of a tree or among ferns.

Crocus A member of the Iris family. This is one of the easiest plants to grow, for it will do equally well in borders, in grass, or in bowls indoors. Put some bone meal in the holes when you plant the corms. Once planted, you can leave them for four years, but then they should be lifted and divided.

1 Forsythia
2 Chionadoxa
3 Christmas Rose
4 Crocus

Daffodil Most Daffodils can be grown in flower borders, in grass, or in bowls indoors. The bulbs should be planted in the autumn. Out-of-doors, large bulbs should be one foot apart and six inches deep; small bulbs six inches apart and one-and-a-half inches deep. They can then be left for five years before being lifted. After flowering, the leaves should be left to yellow off before they are cut.

Narcissus The only difference between a Narcissus and a Daffodil is, as you can see from the picture, that the Narcissus has not got a long trumpet. For planting and growing, the treatment is the same for both.

Tulip Tulips can be grown in flower borders or in bowls indoors, but they will not do well in grass. Put sand and bone meal in the holes when you plant the bulbs in the autumn, six inches deep and five inches apart. They can then be left for three years before lifting. After flowering, allow the leaves to yellow off before removing them.

Primula A member of the Primrose family. This hardy plant is very easy to grow from seed. Most of them prefer a rather damp soil and all of them do better if given some leaf-mould.

1 Daffodil
2 Narcissus
3 Tulip
4 Primula

Iris Reticulata A member of the Iris family, which grows from a bulb. The bulbs should be planted in August or September, in a sunny position, in rich, well-drained soil. Put them six inches apart and three inches deep. They should be lifted and replanted every three years.

Fritillary A member of the Lily family, commonly known as the Snake's-head Lily. The bulbs should be planted four inches deep in the autumn and some sand put in the holes. The Snake's-head Lily grows very well in grass and is also suitable for rockeries.

Polyantha A member of the Primrose family. It flowers in bunches and this distinguishes it from Primulas. The seed should be sown in March in John Innes Compost; the baby plants pricked out in a cold frame and then planted out in June. These should be lifted and replanted in their final positions in September, and can be increased by dividing the roots after flowering. They prefer a moist situation.

Grape Hyacinth A member of the Lily family. The plants are very easy to grow and are especially suitable for rockeries, though they do well in borders. Plant the bulbs in autumn, two inches deep and four inches apart.

1 Iris Reticulata
2 Fritillary
3 Polyantha
4 Grape Hyacinth

Magnolia The Lily-tree. One of the most beautiful of flowering shrubs. The one in the picture flowers in the spring and sheds its leaves for the winter. There are also a few varieties which are evergreen. All Magnolias should be planted in the spring. They need a good loamy soil, and grow better in sheltered positions.

Wallflower Though you may find it difficult to believe, this is a member of the Cabbage family. Deliciously scented, it will thrive on most soils and does not need manuring. Sow the seed in May or June, and when the plants appear, thin them out to one foot apart. Leave them until the autumn and then move them to the flower borders. They will flower the following summer.

Alyssum Another member of the Cabbage family. The dwarf plants are most suitable for rockeries, but they do not like a wet soil. Sow the seeds in March or April and they will flower the same year. Alyssums are perennials.

Forget-Me-Not A native British plant, which does especially well on chalk, but which will thrive on practically any soil in almost any situation. Sow the seeds in early summer. The plants will then be ready for transplanting in the autumn. After flowering, the plants can be increased by splitting them up.

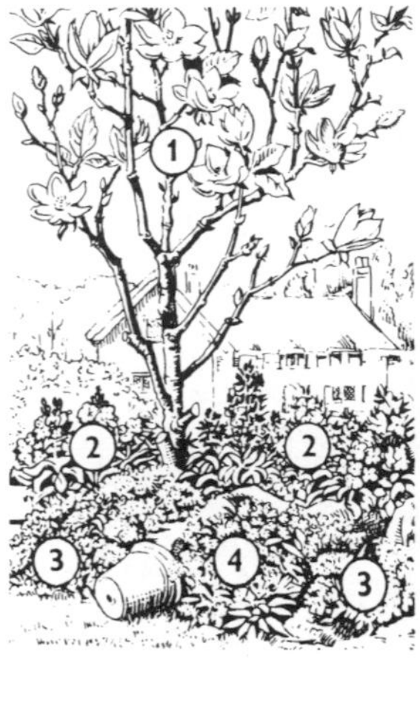

1 Magnolia
2 Wallflower
3 Alyssum
4 Forget-Me-Not

Azalea One of the most brilliant of spring-flowering shrubs, and the leaf colour in the autumn is almost as brilliant. The shrubs like a peaty soil and do best in full sun, but with shelter from neighbouring trees and shrubs. They should be cut back after flowering, but you must get an expert to show you how to do this.

Tulip Here are two more varieties of the plant already described on page 6. These are grown in just the same way. There are a great many varieties of Tulips in all sorts of colours (except blue), so that with care they will bloom from March until late June.

Aubretia A member of the Cabbage family, which is sometimes known as Rock Cress. This is a very hardy, dwarf, evergreen plant, which does splendidly in rockeries or on the margins of flower beds. It produces a mass of bloom in early spring, and then flowers off and on through the summer and into the early autumn. Sow the seed under glass in March or out-of-doors in May.

Arabis Another member of the Cabbage family, which is also sometimes known as Rock Cress. It is cheap to buy and easy to grow, and is excellent for rockeries or for hanging over walls. It will flower in a mild winter, but is at its best in spring when it produces great masses of white bloom. It can easily be increased by division.

1 Azalea
2 Tulip
3 Aubretia
4 Arabis

Iris The name means the " Rainbow Flower ". It is one of the oldest cultivated plants, for its likeness appears on the tombs of the Egyptian Pharoahs. The one in the picture is a Tall Bearded Iris. The rhizomes (which correspond to bulbs in other plants) should be planted in October. Be careful not to bury them. They should be half-out of the soil, in the sunniest possible position. Irises need all the sun they can get. Do not be disappointed if they do not flower for two years. You can increase them by splitting the rhizomes and planting them separately in the autumn.

Peony Though difficult to believe, this is a member of the Buttercup family. It is a hardy perennial which requires good soil and also good staking. Plant in October and remember that Peonies like a fair amount of shade. You can increase by dividing the plants every four years.

Aquilegia Another member of the Buttercup family. Sow the seeds in a frame in spring and transplant them in the summer, when they will flower early in the following year. They are best grown in clumps. Once established they are perennial. They will flourish in almost any soil provided that they are well watered in dry weather.

1 Iris
2 Peony
3 Aquilegia

Lupin Lupins are very hardy plants and will thrive in almost any soil. The seeds should be sown out-of-doors in early summer. They will then flower early in the following year. They are big plants and should be set three to four feet apart. They need staking to prevent them blowing over.

Sweet William A member of the Dianthus family. Sweet Williams are biennials: that is, they should be sown one year to flower the next, and then uprooted. Sow the seed in May. When the plants are transplanted they should be one foot apart. Sweet Williams do best on chalky soil. If the soil is not chalky, they need some lime.

Nigella Also known as Love-in-a-mist. Nigella is a hardy annual: it lives only one year. Sow the seed in spring out-of-doors in ordinary soil and, when the plants appear, thin them out to nine inches apart.

Pansy A member of the Violet family. Pansies are very easy to grow, for they will thrive in almost any soil so long as it is not too dry. The seeds should be sown out-of-doors in early summer. Once you have got Pansies going in your garden, they will seed themselves.

1 Lupin
2 Sweet William
3 Nigella
4 Pansy

Pyrethrum A member of the Chrysanthemum family. Pyrethrums are perennials (come up year after year) and make excellent plants for the flower border, for they will flower a second time if cut back after the first flowering. They can be increased by splitting up the clumps when they start growing.

Cornflower A native British plant which is a hardy annual. Sow the seed out-of-doors in ordinary soil in September or April. When the plants begin to grow, thin them out to one foot apart and stake them, or they may blow over.

Geum A member of the Rose family. Geums will thrive in almost any soil, flower in spring and early summer, and go on flowering for a long time. Sow the seed in boxes in summer to flower the following year. The plants should be set out one-and-a-half feet apart in May.

Stock Some Stocks are biennials and some are annuals. The seed of Brompton Stock, a biennial, should be sown out-of-doors in May to flower the following year. The great thing to remember about Stocks is that they should be planted thickly together.

Day Lily Each flower lasts only a day, but the plant will go on flowering for a very long time. Day Lilies are best planted in clumps one foot apart in a sunny position. They can be increased by splitting up the clumps in spring.

1 Pyrethrum *2 Cornflower*
3 Geum *4 Stock*
5 Day Lily

Hybrid Tea Rose The H.T. Roses, of which there are many varieties, are a modern development. Many are beautifully scented. They thrive on any well-drained soil, but need annual manuring. They are best planted in the autumn, and require hard pruning in the spring, at the end of March or early in April. Pruning is an art, and it is better to get an expert to show you how to do it the first time.

Floribunda Rose The name given to all those Roses which flower in clusters, having many flowers at the same time. They are very hardy and should be planted in the autumn. They do not require as hard pruning as the H.T. Roses, but again it is best to get an expert to show you how to do it.

Lavender A shrub famous for its scent. It will flourish on most soils, but is particularly fond of chalk. Plant two feet apart, either in the autumn or spring. You can get more plants by taking cuttings of the side shoots during the growing season.

Dianthus This is the Carnation family. The flowers in the picture are the very popular hybrids known as Allwoodii. The seed should be sown out-of-doors in summer. Once the plants are established, they can be increased by pulling young shoots out of the sockets of the old plants, and replanting them in sandy, moist soil in summer.

1 Hybrid Tea Rose
2 Floribunda Rose
3 Lavender
4 Dianthus

Delphinium A member of the Buttercup family. A tall perennial plant which flowers from June onwards. Delphiniums can be grown from seed, but it is better to get young plants. They require rich, well-drained soil and a sunny, but sheltered, position.

Gaillardia A member of the Daisy family. There are annual and perennial varieties. It is better to start with the annuals, which can be easily grown from seed. Sow the seed in the spring in light, fertile soil, and the plants will bloom profusely in the summer.

Gypsophila A hardy perennial, which will grow into a broad bush and is sometimes known as the " Chalk Plant ". It is easily raised from seed sown in the spring, and will thrive in most soils, though it particularly likes chalk.

Eschscholtzia A member of the Poppy family, this is the Californian Poppy. It is an annual plant which is very easy to grow from seed sown in boxes in early spring, or sown out-of-doors in April. The plants should be set out one foot apart in May in well-dug soil.

Canterbury Bell This is a biennial plant which will do well in any well-dug soil. Sow the seed thinly out-of-doors in May, and set the plants out two feet apart in the autumn, when they will flower the following year. The plants need staking. Pick off the fading flowers and many more blooms will grow.

1 Delphinium 2 Gaillardia
3 Gypsophila 4 Eschscholtzia
5 Canterbury Bell

Allium A member of the Lily family. There are many varieties, all with beautiful flowers, but they all require a sunny position and well-drained soil, and do best on rockeries. The seed should be sown in a cold frame in spring.

Pink One of the real old-fashioned garden flowers which has never lost its popularity. The white variety, known as Mrs. Sinkins, is perhaps the best known. The seed should be sown out-of-doors in summer, but once the plants are established, they can be increased by pulling the young shoots out of the sockets of the old plants, and re-planting them in sandy soil out-of-doors in summer.

Saxifrage There is an enormous variety of Saxifrages. Some of them are very small and moss-like in their growth, while others are quite tall, loose and spreading. They are all hardy alpine plants, and most of them are very suitable for rockeries. It is best to plant in the autumn.

Lithospermum A dwarf, evergreen, creeping shrub which produces a wealth of bright blue flowers in early summer. It is particularly suitable for rockeries. It is sometimes known as Gromwell.

Armeria Commonly known as Thrift, this is a native British plant. There are a great many garden varieties, which are particularly suited to sunny positions in the rockery.

Gentian A hardy alpine plant which is best grown in rockeries or in old sinks. The one in the picture is called Acaulis, and it likes a gravel soil. Gentians are said to be difficult to grow, but this is because they are often planted in unsuitable soil.

1 Allium *2 Pink*
3 Saxifrage *4 Lithospermum*
5 Armeria *6 Gentian*

Lily The national flower of France. The ones in the picture are all out-door Lilies. *L. Auratum*, from Japan, likes plenty of leaf-mould and a certain amount of shade. The others all like the sun, but want their roots shaded, so it is a good thing to put them among other plants. *L. Regale*, from China, is easy to grow and reaches a height of six feet. *L. Martagon*, about three feet high, is also easy to grow and flowers freely. *L. Tigrinum*, the Tiger Lily, four feet high, flowers in September, which is later than the others. Lily bulbs should be planted in the autumn in holes filled with sand five inches deep and six inches apart. After flowering, do not cut the flower stems down until they are yellow.

Meconopsis A member of the Poppy family. The one in the picture is the famous Blue Poppy of Tibet. It is a very hardy perennial. Sow the seed in August, in soil with plenty of leaf-mould. *M. Cambrica*, the Welsh Poppy, has yellow flowers and is even hardier.

1 Lily
2 Meconopsis

Achillea A member of the Daisy family, often known as Yarrow. It is one of the easiest plants to grow, for it is hardy and does not mind what sort of soil it grows in. In fact, it will do well on heavy, cold ground. You can increase the plants by dividing them in autumn or spring.

Alstromeria The Peruvian Lily. Though hardy, it grows best in a sunny, sheltered position and prefers sandy soil. If you remove the flowers as soon as they fade you will get blooms practically throughout the summer. You can increase the plants by division in the autumn, but you should not do it every year.

Anchusa A hardy perennial which grows vigorously in cool moist places. It does not need a rich soil. Sow the seed in the spring for flowering the following year; or the plants can be increased by division in the autumn.

Helenium A member of the Daisy family and another very easy plant to grow, for it is hardy and will do well in any good garden soil, flowering in late summer. It is easy to grow from seed, and can also be increased by division in the spring.

1 *Achillea*
2 *Alstromeria*
3 *Anchusa*
4 *Helenium*

Kniphofia A member of the Lily family, commonly known as " Red-hot Poker ". Start by sowing seed in spring, but once the plants have grown, the roots can be divided in spring to get more plants. Kniphofia does best in rich soil. In the autumn the long leaves must be tied in knots, and let them wither before snapping them off.

Gladiolus A member of the Iris family. It is best to start by buying corms (bulbs), for the seeds take two years to flower. Plant the corms one foot apart in a sunny position, and put some sand and peat or leaf-mould in the holes. The plants must be staked. In November lift the corms and store them in a box of sand for use the following year.

Carnation A member of the Dianthus family. It is best to start with some of the border varieties, which are evergreens. Get young plants in spring and plant them one and a half feet apart in deeply-dug soil, putting some ashes in the holes. Each plant must be staked.

Lobelia The dwarf one shown in the picture is the best to start with, for it makes a wonderful edging for flower beds, and will bloom for several months. Sow the seed in a frame in the winter. Once you have plants you can increase them by taking cuttings in the autumn, but you must grow the cuttings in pots.

1 Kniphofia
2 Gladiolus
3 Carnation
4 Lobelia

Nasturtium Climbing Nasturtiums should be grown against a wall or on a pergola. The smaller varieties do well in ornamental urns, as shown in the picture, or at the front of flower borders. They are very easy to grow, but do not like rich soil. Sow the seed outside in spring to flower in the summer. When the plants appear, thin them to nine inches apart.

Hollyhock There are perennial and annual Hollyhocks. It is best to start with the annual varieties. Sow the seeds under glass towards the end of winter, and set the plants out in June, when they will flower in July or August. They need staking, and do especially well against a fence or wall.

Geranium The plants shown in the picture are called Pelargoniums. They can only be grown in pots. Geraniums can be taken from their pots in June and set out in the flower borders, but really these are greenhouse plants, and they cannot be grown successfully without a greenhouse.

Antirrhinum A native British plant, commonly called " Snapdragon ". Sow the seed under glass in March. When the baby plants appear, prick them out three inches apart and allow them plenty of air. Set them out in May one foot apart and they will flower before midsummer.

1 Nasturtium
2 Hollyhock
3 Geranium
4 Antirrhinum

Echinops This is the Globe Thistle, a hardy perennial plant which grows about three feet high and blooms in the summer. It is very easy to grow in any ordinary garden soil, and the plants can be increased by dividing the roots in spring.

Anemone Japonica A member of the Buttercup family. The variety shown in the picture blooms in late summer and autumn. To start with, a plant must be bought, but after that the only difficulty is keeping it within bounds. It spreads very rapidly and, if the plant is not kept under strict control, will soon swamp other plants and even force its way up through gravel paths.

Coleus This is an evergreen shrub which is valued for its coloured leaves, the flowers being quite insignificant. Though Coleus can be put out in the border for the summer, as shown in the picture, they are really greenhouse or conservatory plants, and cannot be kept through the winter unless the plants are potted-up and placed in a warm greenhouse.

Begonia This is another plant which cannot really be managed without a greenhouse, for it must be grown in a pot in heat until May. Begonias can then be planted out in June, in rich soil, in a fairly shady position. After flowering they must be lifted in September, and the tubers (which correspond to bulbs) stored in a dry place for the winter, potting them up again in the spring.

1 Echinops
2 Anemone Japonica
3 Coleus
4 Begonia

Clematis A member of the Buttercup family. Clematis are beautiful climbing plants, which can be grown up walls or over a trellis or a tree stump. They need good, rich soil with plenty of manure, and a sunny position. They are best planted in autumn and should be given plenty of water in the spring.

Climbing Rose The true Climbing and Rambler Roses are Polyantha Roses, which grow vigorously and bear abundant clusters of single or double flowers. They are excellent for growing up pillars, over arches, or against walls. They need scarcely any pruning, but the dead flowers should always be removed.

Passion Flower A beautiful climber which blooms in summer, not really hardy and must be planted in a sheltered position. A good idea is to cut back the side shoots to one inch from the base in February. The plant gets its name because the various parts resemble the articles used at the crucifixion of Christ. The leaf is the spear; the tendrils, the scourges; the column, the pillar of the Cross; the anthers, the hammer; the styles, the nails. The white signifies purity and the blue, heaven.

Ipomoea A member of the Convolvulus family, commonly known as "Morning Glory". The best are the annuals, which are easily grown from seed. Sow the seed in a frame in spring and plant out, using plenty of sand, for summer flowering.

1 Clematis
2 Climbing Rose
3 Passion Flower
4 Ipomoea

Pelargonium The one shown in the picture is the Ivy-leaved Pelargonium. Like the Geranium described on page 32, it can only be grown in a pot (when it must be trained up stakes) or in a hanging basket. The basket may be put out-of-doors from June to September, but must be brought in for the winter.

Agapanthus This is the African Lily from the Cape of Good Hope. It is not hardy and so is best grown in a large tub, so that it can be moved indoors for the winter. You can get more plants by division in spring.

Amaryllis Belladonna The Belladonna Lily. Another tub plant which may be placed out-of-doors in a sheltered position in September, but must be brought in for the winter. The bulbs should be planted in a compost of three parts loam to one part leaf-mould and one quarter part sand. The leaves come after the beautiful flowers.

Carpentaria An evergreen shrub which grows to ten feet high and bears scented flowers in June. Any garden soil suits it, but it must have the shelter of a wall, if it is to survive the winter.

Petunia A member of the Potato family. It is an annual, which likes a sunny position and bears a profusion of brilliant flowers. Any soil will do, but it must be kept well-watered. The dead heads should be picked off to encourage further flowering. It is best to buy plants (which are cheap) and to set them one foot apart.

1 Pelargonium 2 Agapanthus
3 Amaryllis Belladonna
4 Carpentaria 5 Petunia

Foxglove This is a biennial, which means that you should sow the seed one year to give flowering plants the next. But, as a matter of fact, once you have got Foxgloves you need not bother to sow seed, because they seed themselves freely, and you will find them popping up all over the place.

Periwinkle This is a hardy evergreen, which is valuable in the garden because it will grow under trees and in other shady places where most plants will not grow. Moreover, it is not a bit particular about the sort of soil. You can get more plants by division in the spring.

Solomon's Seal This is another plant which likes shady places, but it will not grow actually under trees. It is wonderfully graceful and very hardy, but is slow growing. It is best planted in the autumn.

St. John's Wort There are many varieties of this hardy perennial. One of the most popular is sometimes known as the " Rose of Sharon ". It will grow almost anywhere (even under trees) and is practically evergreen. It should be planted one foot apart in the autumn, and it will then form a dense mass.

1 Foxglove
2 Periwinkle
3 Solomon's Seal
4 St. John's Wort

Sunflower A member of the Daisy family. The one shown in the picture is the Common Sunflower, which is a hardy annual, growing to a height of six to ten feet. It is easily grown from seeds sown one quarter of an inch deep in ordinary soil, in a sunny position, where desired to flower.

Phlox One of the most magnificent perennial garden plants. It will thrive in any good soil, but needs plenty of watering. Phloxes are easy to grow from seed sown in frames in summer, and the plants can be increased by division at any time between November and April.

Michaelmas Daisy There is an enormous variety of Michaelmas Daisies in many different colours and heights. All are hardy perennials and flower when most other garden plants are past their best. They are easy to grow in almost any soil, and can be increased by division in spring just when they begin to grow. Plants which have stood for two years should always be divided.

Montbretia A South African plant which does well in sunny borders in well-drained soil. Plant the bulbs three inches deep and two inches apart in March or April, with a little sand in the holes. There is nothing else required for propagation.

1 Sunflower
2 Phlox
3 Michaelmas Daisy
4. Montbretia

Chrysanthemum This is the " Golden Flower " of the Chinese. The perennial varieties are in bloom through the summer from May to October. The annual varieties are easy to grow from seed and flower in a few weeks. The annuals are especially good for indoor decoration. Both sorts will flourish in sunny positions in any good garden soil.

Zinnia Zinnias are annuals of most brilliant colours. They should be planted in June, and until they begin to grow should be sheltered from the wind. A bit of sacking will do this very well. They grow very fast, and must then be tied to a good stake or they will blow over.

Limonium Bonduelli A member of the Plumbago family. The one in the picture comes from Algeria and is an annual. It has to be grown in pots indoors (the seed should be sown in February) and then transplanted out-of-doors in May. It must have a sunny position.

1 Chrysanthemum
2 Zinnia
3 Limonium Bonduelli

Golden Rod A member of the Daisy family. It will thrive in any soil and either in sun or shade. Sow the seed out-of-doors in April. The plants can be increased by splitting the roots in winter, but this will probably not be necessary, as Golden Rod often spreads so quickly that it becomes almost a weed.

Dahlia Another member of the Daisy family, which came originally from Mexico. There are a great many different sorts, but all require a deep, fertile and moist soil. All Dahlias, to flower properly, require a lot of watering during the growing stage. Dahlias can be grown from seed, but it is better to start by buying plants in the spring for delivery in June. The tubers (corresponding to bulbs in other plants) should be lifted in the autumn and stored for the winter in a dry, frost-proof place, for replanting the following year. If this is done, each plant will last for several years.

Helichrysum Another member of the Daisy family, commonly known as the " Everlasting Flower " The seeds should be sown in boxes in February, and the plants set out one-and-a-half feet apart in May. If the flowers are gathered early and hung head downwards in bunches in a cool, dry place, the colour will remain throughout the winter.

1 Golden Rod
2 Dahlia
3 Helichrysum

Philadelphus A member of the Saxifrage family. Often called Syringa or Mock Orange. This is a beautiful and very hardy shrub with a wonderful scent. It will thrive in any ordinary soil. After flowering all the old wood should be cut out.

Hibiscus A member of the Mallow family. The one in the picture is Syriacus, a hardy shrub which blooms late in summer and seems to do particularly well near towns. You can increase the plants by taking cuttings and planting them in sand, with leaf-mould, in a cold frame. They should be planted out in the autumn.

Hydrangea A member of the Saxifrage family. Because of their large heads of bloom, Hydrangeas are very popular as pot plants indoors, and many people think of them only as indoor plants. There are hardy outdoor ones as well, but, as a matter of fact, many of the pot plants will do perfectly well out-of-doors, if they are planted as soon as they have finished flowering.

1 Philadelphus
2 Hibiscus
3 Hydrangea

INDEX OF GARDEN FLOWERS

Series 536